This Journal Belongs To

_____

_____

_____

For spiral bound journals (personalized and non-personalized) and other products with this and other designs, please visit us at our Etsy shop.
www.nimblemuseprintables.etsy.com

If you have enjoyed this publication and found it useful, we would be grateful if you would leave us a review.
Thank you.

Made in the USA
Middletown, DE
28 May 2022